Solarium

poems

Jordan Zandi

SARABANDE BOOKS LOUISVILLE, KY

Library of Congress Cataloging-in-Publication Data
Zandi, Jordan, 1984-
 [Poems. Selections]
Solarium / Jordan Zandi. -- First edition.
    pages cm.
"Winner of the 2014 Kathryn A. Morton Prize in Poetry ; selected by Henri Cole."
ISBN 978-1-941411-17-9 (paperback) -- ISBN 978-1-941411-18-6 (ebook)
I. Title.
PS3626.A6295A6 2016
811'.6--dc23

                    2015017013

Cover design and interior by Kristen Radtke.
Manufactured in Canada.
This book is printed on acid-free paper.

Sarabande Books is a nonprofit literary organization.

The Kentucky Arts Council, the state arts agency, supports Sarabande Books with state tax dollars and federal funding from the National Endowment for the Arts.

For my parents.
And for Louise.

Contents

IV

Foreword

Solarium is a completely original gem of a book. I have never met Jordan Zandi, but I would like to, for there is a sweet spirit haunting his guileless poems. "The Poetry of earth is never dead," Keats wrote in his psychological sonnet "On the Grasshopper and Cricket," and with their muddy rivers, fecund fields, and train horns in the distance, Zandi's poems seem to bear this out. Landscape is never mechanical or dead in his work but vitally connected to his mind, where his poems originate in the darker passages of feeling, but his love of nature leads him to an awakened consciousness.

Solarium feels like an American book, though not because of its Midwestern-small-town locale. More because of the way the spiritual dilemmas of everyday life lead Zandi to exclamatory acts of the mind. The unusual, unified vision of this book is one in which the thinking-feeling man—disconnected and morose ("I was a dead thing once," Zandi writes)—finds refuge in the language of a fable-like place, a kind of archetypal Utopia where there is mournfulness, anxiety, and self-doubt (can one ever really escape these things?), but also the endless orgy of the seasons in which Zandi's poems continually find delight, with their rose gardens and earth smells, their damp forests and frozen lakes, their deer and hounds, their silos, cherry trees, and shaggy fungi.

It isn't exactly optimism I hear in the playful surfaces and linguistic frivolity of Zandi's poems, but a quiet hopefulness, the kind of hopefulness that cannot be seen but is a way of locating oneself in relation to a difficult past. His inner world is always interacting with the outer world, and as a result everything seems to be shining. The sun is coming up and he is leading his companion-horse slowly through deep woods to drink and refresh herself at the river's edge.

"Walking across the binary field, / What does the young man see?" Zandi asks, searching for signs with his subtle eyes. The answer seems to be the great opium of simply being content within oneself—with a heart that receives and watches (if a heart watches), while resisting the systems that hurt us—and remaining awake to experience.

—Henri Cole

I

I, the dreamer . . .

—William Faulkner

On Stepping off the Train

Ta Da.   You go out.

Shocked fully into normal.
Winter: isn't silent. Snows are dragging.

And there is the lake you stood by
standing under granite set in the hills

steadfast

the leaves stuck on the water's suspension
an insect fastened to the line, worn out
the worn-out reeds bending
leaves rustling on the lake and shifting.

Bowl of the lake. Bowl of the sky.
Bowl of the lake with the sky in it.

You looked at you in the water.

The blizzard is cold.
And the boy in the blizzard is blue.

On My Path Life

It was the night, or would be, and the horse was carrying me down the lane of pines. The night was winterless and the song between us was being sung; us, the horse and I, old friend who carried me now as always through forest damp this distance to the same dark place. *When you get there, what will you plant there?* But it was not for her to know; and if I had to talk about my life I would say it was like that.

A bend, and then another, so that the forest that had seemed the same took on two shapes. She stopped there—and spoke without finishing—to turn and look back down for the road, toward the place where the evergreens shut.

From a Bridge

I remember the river rising. It must have

been nearly fall, the banked earth's

smell like a late yellow above the water's

slow upward climb. That river was so muddy

you'd never wade it this time of year

but even so, boys from the town would jump

off bridges, thinking maybe the depth

was safer, but they were wrong. My mother

told me a story once of her father, how he

was like those boys and jumped off bridges.

When the long rains came the water rose

that year also, but the bottom shifted

as the currents changed, thus when he dove

he broke his neck. And then not

paralyzed, he dragged his head

from the muck, swimming to the bank

on which he could lay his body down,

not be carried out to sea.

The Gift Horse

You can lead a horse to water
but when the blind lead the blind
he who hesitates is lost.

Every field looks green from this distance,
even this cemetery, though the grass
on the other side feels greener.
I ride slowly—it gets me just as far—
through the country where the one-eyed man
is king. My blind companion, Curiosity,
my dark horse, is music on the journey.
I hear them, changing horses in the middle of streams.
At times, I tell them: better to ask twice than lose the way once.
At other times, silent, I pass for a philosopher.
Don't worry when you stumble, I tell myself;
the worm is the only thing that can't fall down.

The Flavor Suite

Three quarks for Muster Mark!

—James Joyce

I   Spin 1

Because if I had
six elements, I too
would call them Up,
Down, Bottom, Top,
Charm, and Strange:

II   Riddle

and am a useful tool
perhaps, like an anvil
though also the hammer,
am an answer
for a kind of play and capable
of containing forest,
mountain,
sea:

5

III   Spin 2

and so I spin this ball
in hand—I mean
my fingers spin

—and stand asking
myself why would I
do that to myself?

IV   Sea

Call death a sea. I say
there's nothing like the sea
in me.

Solarium

1

      And daybreak! The sun
sitting up—

          Oh God
          I thought I saw God spread out
          in the roses again—

Momentarily,
I will be taken up
like flame in a cloud like a cinder in fire
               to outflap the empyrean—

Dead things gumming the sidewalk.
Hello,
      dead things.

Tell me: what good is a life that wears away?

2

I chew the red wire,
           then the blue wire.
Then through the flowered wallpaper—

Oh! Look at this charming table:
already set; built for a mouse;

and silent as a banquet hall
after the guests have gone.

3

I was a dead thing once.

On the back porch once—
      facing the square
of my mother's rose-
      garden, with the northfacing windows
full-opened in June, and other flowers,
      the names I've forgotten, all gone
into bloom,
      I've heard the train horn bawl out again
from across the river, first sound
      I remember, tolled
through the walls of an empty house,

have watched the coyotes come loping
across these frost-flocked rows of the field—

4

"Quick—to the window, Mother
come see—the coyote,
he's dragging a haunch by the bone."

8

He'll lay it down, lie down
beside it, then sink
his teeth in the flitch.

5

The dream is big, the dream is fancy:
the dream is big and fancy.
The rodent: cuddly; but a little dirty.
I'll keep him as a pet, I'll pet him like
a luck-charm—

6

Remember summers, Jordan?
Eating quinces, spitting the seeds?
And how you never ate quinces again
when they laughed when you called them quinces?
And now there are no more quinces?

I do remember quinces.

7

Beautiful ones—I see you everywhere.
Hiding inside yourselves.

8

Sometimes time is iron. Swing it hard
hear it *whoosh*.

9

At the door, the red curtain is still flapping.
Who will go in?

The one who is going
is going.

No, I do not die here.
The year is wrong.

Earth returns
and today no cloud cover.

I wish my heart was as big as the world,
but bigger—

10

The sun sitting up
        ever so slowly—

Epic

—At the door, the red curtain is still flapping.
Who will go in?

The cedar chips have stayed with me;
also these mint tea leaves;
and the tiger-rock from Yumani.

In the Opposite Rooms

A man not willing to climb
steps into the room that
has no stairs or ladders
wearing attire both smart
and sharp—a gray suit perhaps—
and his hair is reasonable.

I know this because I wear it
as if I were speaking into a mirror
—and no one was listening—
of how a man not willing to climb
trees came to be
here, in the opposite rooms

and this was how I came to possess your body.

On My Painting Life

Once there was a man with no name who could read and write who spoke very well with big accents. Once, there was an avocado on his plate, a dead fish; then three spiky seeds.

This one lived in a cave, where he fashioned a jamboree of creatures to populate his wall-length. His bison crept on thresholds over stone shelves, and moon-eyed fish leapt free of cold cave-streams, though sometimes light from the fire spliced his shadow on the wall, obscured them.

And he watched as outside, naked and wooly, one mammoth caterpillar crawled a tree-limb, once. Its journey, round and round, brought him round earth's meridian, whence he found this objective: the other wall.

II

Once I asked Daddy if there was a place in the sky where the sky is what is hard and the place where trees are is all wind, an upside-down world like when I close my eyes on the tractor. He said it was a good question.

—Peter Reich

River

On a trestle bridge in late summer, thighs together,
back pressed warmly to her back, dangling
legs down through the slats, hot on the black metal

we lounged together, listening to river birds, wind-play through trees;
I held a stick, she hummed, while I thoughtlessly drummed with it.
Below, the Wabash churned its foam around the stanchions.

We talked of nothing I remember,
or we laughed and talked of nothing,
until the sun tucked down.

That's the past, she's married now. I sit in my chair,
trying to turn back toward these things. Outside,
the cars rush past, through the glass sounding nothing like water.

Adjustments

Young, I expected violences:
peal of the storm-sheared oak, the
rabbit's shriek from the underbrush.

Though years have flaked from me
lichen still molds to stone.

Now in the fold sheep drowse
while at the river's mouth
twin deer are drinking.

Le Monde Familier

A cabin stands, deserted, on a beach.

—Wallace Stevens

Where once there was no
material, material begins

an island-president: an exile
then, whose day's events

>   *(to sit on log,*
>   *to clean off bark)*

to make the green
stone an axe-head
joined to a well-
balanced shaft
and *sharp* (as
the axe-head
called itself)
succeeded only now.

●

Shaving the bark it felt
as if I only smoothed it from the log
under the blade's whetted petting

    (and soon this house
    will open to the sun)

while beyond it: the white sea
and the stone in the sky
and the cloud in the sky

covered the familiar world.

An Island Journal

The First Day

So tired . . . after the swimming . . . like part of me walks behind
me.

Day the Fourth

Tell me, coconut, what was the water like?

The Sixth Day

Beginning to make great leaps across the island

—why, birds have gawked at me.

#14

I am like shadow, dark as a wing,
am darker than shadow, when tensed like a wing.

July 14th

Do I put this feather with the darkness
or the darkness with the wind?

Day After the Last

My hand in the water glass—
The willow-stripling put out roots!

The Last Day

Black birdsong. The hand falls.
They *thip* into the sea.

On My Pool Life

Although the pool was empty, during the many years before the man would stay in his pool all day, steeping himself like a bag of tea, until one day he was filled with a loud wanting. He cupped both hands to cover his ears. Above, the clouds bestirred themselves, threatening rain. "What is it you want?" he wanted to shout, just like his father once did from the garden, shaking his wooden trowel at the sky. But the clouds came on, gathering like inverted heads over the crowns of the cherries, while around the garden beyond, the old railroad ties, which had loosened, still lay where they lay.

Chamber Music

1

No one knows where the storm came from.

2

Scratching their heads—the weathermen. The satellites
bungled the news. Clumsy
instruments. Then somebody said:

It's just a projection.

3

Yet hadn't the dog in its doghouse howled;
and didn't the cat jump down from the roof?

4

Inside mangroves a man docks his boat.
Inside his cabin he rides in a storm.
He opens the bottle of wine.

Outside, the storm peeks in through the porthole.
And the wind is frisking.

5

Here is what else a storm's eye sees:
it doesn't say much

      but it sees me.

With a ukulele. Having a memory.

6

Pink and cheap—the ukulele.

Although the storm

7

—it changes nothing.

Sting of the sky's electric string-release!

Which changes nothing.

8

Was I the man with wine and a boat?
I wasn't the man with wine and a boat

but the boy on the dock
was me.

Acrylic I

This grove between the houses:
fake plastic birds on a tiny pine;
pinwheels, spinning, turn then stand.

While he is out tending to hedges,
everything shines
like the back of your hand.

Etch-a-Sketch

There you are.
In that junkyard.

Come closer, little memory—I'll let you in on a secret.
You lose your virginity here.

Closer, little memory—what did you find
on your treasure hunt?

So cold.

So soon
a blackness creeps   across the moon, as if
the head was turning
on a hinge.

Butterfly knife. A pocket watch.

Your throat gorged on goneforever.

Vector

A good time, a trying time—up on the branch
the cat falls.

The tree falls.
It's quiet as grass
trying to grow.

Goodbye, favorite tree.

Halls, Then Banquet

They carried me out on a gurney.
Doctor's orders:
lie in bed, listen
to the wind thump ground.

      Nights were long.

Those
thunks of a cane
retreating further down the corridor . . .
then orderlies' footsteps.

Did I say I was in hospital?
I *was* in hospital,
only much younger than originally
I'd thought. Asthma again,
and the cold
washcloth not enough
to cut the fevers.

I remember white squares,
a hole in the ceiling
from which, over and over, a silver
droplet fell.

When I finally came home . . .
Seeing the same figs! Your napkin on the table.

On My Pony Life

No one gave me a pony. I want a pony, so someone could lead me around. I have endured. On my pony I would carry a lolly, its colors in a spiral. Not all the colors, but those at least of the rainbow. Someone would say "How smart you are" as they began to thread ribbons in the tail.

III

To strive to become what one already is: who would take the pains to waste his time on such a task?

—Kierkegaard

The Circus in Winter

I.

What moves things, she asked.
The wind, he replied.

~

I found the red bird: the robin
with the red breast, still tilting
on the limb, who *heehees* for the spring.

O perching V's! What he's drawing
are birds. Above the horizon,
where the sun has rested its nose,
its big eyes, big, for a sun

the sheepish clouds are smiling
their sheep-like bodies, and the tree
—where the spider is drifting, out
to the center, the figure, rather exultant
of the man—says, *I look like broccoli.*

It's okay to tell the child
his birds move south in the winter.
Every winter, I searched
in the frost-locked tree, I gave it beads
and ornaments, I dangled lights around it,
and the tree was comfort.

II.

Come again, my friend. Today
I want you to make me sad. Today
I will make you sad.

~

Peru. Not that one.
You wouldn't mistake it.
Our silos—No, they are nothing
but silos. Very good for storing.

I believed: in nymphs in the forest;
in the garden-shepherds our gnomes.

(Sometimes, through the window, the sun made much of me)

When pain becomes, "becomes the whole
environment of the night":

machinery.

And here I see the gazelle leap out
under the swatch of the lion's paw,
imperial, like thought
unable to arrest itself.

III.

The Circus in Winter.
Yes horse, let's go there.

~

Walking across the binary field,
what does the young man see?
(His head chock-full of irony)

That winter, as deer pursued our hounds
with teeth transpiring flame, expiring sounds
of autumn scuffed down alleyways . . .

Cloud-damp, in yellow dungarees,
he of the yellow spring arrives:
adjusts the gas to fit intent.

The clink of silver on the kettle.
Drip.
Seasons were a way of putting it.

Now answer, question, or answer
nothing.
Then trowel to the next section.

IV.

nayra (eye) or
nayra (before)—
chasing the cone of light . . .

~

A life spent
        going out and never into—

V.

It'll be warm on the mountain?
We'll be closer to the sun.

~

So much for childhood.

Occupied, for years,
        with the drawing of these fingers
                and their rubbing, over and through
the guts of the fish
decanting these omens,
                up in the lighthouse, I watched
        (as phrases rose, "fresh from the
undersurging") my heart
attach to feeling, this
                genome heart, Red Country—
until
        "there came new subtlety of eyes
                into my tent:"
        I had not seen the
odd insects, trees, and rolling dune sands
                (for a long time) halting
        at a great fresh water—no shells,
there is just plain, soft sand. At night

the water striders skate the lake
        like four-pointed
stars, shifting across the water.

Then moving inland,
going by broken-down stalls for horses,
>   *a spirit passed before my face,*
>   *the hair of my flesh stood up;*
and certain birds can hear this,
>   a sound in the dark the dark makes
when the dark rebounds.

Quarry

I found myself by the lake, below the first house.
A curiosity had called me there, the pond
snails at the edge the size of buckeyes; and those
in reach dropped softly to the bucket, while others,
farther off, wound algae at a dark edge
between, or bit slow trails through bottom worlds,
so sometimes, when I'd circled back around
they'd be there, ready to hand. Then trudging,
a little muddy, up the hill, stopping between gardens,
the slate around the lake below still slightly dis-
lodged and interspersed with dolostone,
limestone, shale, I'd see the silver maple,
sycamore, and cherry flash silver, their leaves
upturned by wind—and there were
crows among them sleeping! and green
mantises, and under the stones the Armadillidiidae.

IV

When the warm days do arrive, though, the taiga blooms, and for a few short months it can seem almost welcoming. It is then that man can see most clearly into this hidden world—not on land, for the taiga can swallow whole armies of explorers, but from the air.

—Mike Dash

Snow Children

The one who wrote that the sun going down
might be a subject of praise, the one
who wrote that the same coming up
might be a subject of praise . . .

—I have said less than I intended.

Watching snow children, so squat
in fat coats, their joy as instant
as a stone that leaves the hand—
I remember clouds migrating
overhead, and the road that leads
out of the pine wood's margins.
Then snow, more snow . . .

—the only kind of it.

All Around the Garden of the Gods

All around the garden of the gods, the gods were growing:
this one with annoying fruit and that one with alarming leaves.
In one corner was a pine cone, whose shingles smiled.
In others shaggy funguses, with heads like purple wigs
stuck out of the ground. And a shagbark, her branches filled
with orange eggs, stood over a deer whose mossy antlers
cut the wind. The various constructions to employ the mind
thudding into wall. the wall. the wall. the wall slanting
that direction in which all gardens of the gods reside.

A Lesson in Botany

Meadow-empty: first the dark
and now this moon flows on me.
All over feels like a wetness.

You are a common place, and I a tree.
I am no place at all.

Yet there is an echo
out of your hollow. What makes a place?

Empty is not one, Meadow.

***

Some have observed that even the trees dream.
I say that mostly a tree dreams.

What would meadows be dreaming of?

Of being a sea. Of things that move
but stay to the earth. To be young,
to be old. Which we express
like this: he has grown out
to encompass that post;
and he will grow into his.

***

One can be borne
either smooth (wind)
or rough (bird).

Rough. Like with knobs—Is this a riddle?
You have many.

Like with knobs.

Wind is a long thing, too thin to see.

Like precision or loneliness.

These things also grow through us.
You are my trunk.

And you are the length
beneath me.

***

Withhold fire, meadows grow old. Brush
then a bush then a tree
then trees: that place is gone.

If fire makes me, what makes trees?

***

"Oxbow."

That one bends in on itself.

Bend in, you bend away from what is out.

For a river, a bend is a way of leaving.

For a river, the leaving is living.

***

Yesterday, a cloud. Today
there are two.

You didn't see the one behind me.

Saw your branches growing darker,
thought it was anger.

Clouds become what they've become before.

And after?

You see the blue come poking through my branches.

Last Beach Motel

As verdigris room reflects
   Sister Moon, my brother stands

where iron bars once striped
   or gripped his face. He must

go out soon. So walking across
   calm indices of sands beneath

pale cumulonimbi the moon
   draws into frame, he does

go out. This beach's palms
   wave in the wind like fronds

on parrot shirts; the tourist hum's
   all gone into yesterday and beyond

the tympanic drum of the waves
   thumping a lone buoy

into the keel of a moored
   rowboat. He would get in

but instead, chooses to see
   jostled in the line of surf

a thing let go of its anatomy
   in a green mesh of sea blades,

kelp, the limbs of the sea, which even
   there, starving by moonlight,

glowed amber and embryonic.

On My So-Called *Life*

The objects now gathered, one each day, stack high as sky or a ceiling. When I needed more room I struck out a wall, and conveniently, found another. And objects within each other: the tree had drunk the river, the elephants swallowed trombones—their trunks played on and on. Today it's over. Any sentence could be the last, last thought of the month. But tomorrow, I may repass this wealth of rooms; so the band plays on and on.

Inside

1

As loud as cats—and happiness!
Such happiness ran through the walls

and she affirmed it
over and over; oh—yes!
She affirmed it!

Sounds were rolling around the room;
the pots and pans sang off the shelf.

2

What happened to her happiness?

It ran away?

Or somebody stole her happiness?

3

Listen.

You want to hold yourself together?
Buy a rope.

You want to keep your life together?
Buy a fence.

4

Not even the neighbors know I'm here.

On My Plane Life

All of us were headed north. I was in a plane—I felt the all-around bounce of it. Being in a plane, like love, may require you get close to someone you sometimes hate. I couldn't wait to go. I thought of love and planes, and love on planes—then slept, coasting among white clouds, and mind was my atmosphere.

Riddle

Regular hills and bent trees
front the mountain.
Above the mountain
are more clouds
and when it gets dark
those clouds turn into
mountains, so the land
once reaching up
starts reaching out
into a sky
that had seemed like ocean
cooling to black
while even now, row
by row repeating
the waves around me
move onward. If there
is a path beneath the waves
then surely that bottom
may tell us something, is
the reflection of something; that bottom
which is desert, and the mountain
which is desert.

—So sat with it, beneath
stone monuments. Egyptian
I think. Some
Era. I see
in the bottom
like ridged sky rising
out of the blank sand
an eternal fan-
rotation of hours

I'll never have
done with. By evening
I look for a road.

Transparencies

His father though a tall man
contained his tallness, carried
himself in himself, like a jar,
a small jar made of just glass

and smallness; as to his mother
she saw the inside-strings of everything
she touched, made faucets sing
growing her gardens rough.

Father come home at night
in the doorway: "I don't see into things,"
he would say, and Mother would see
that the glass was working.

At the Sign of the Skull

At the reservoir
I saw it first, said

we'd show the vet
who said, "Small dog."

The waiting room held
canine hearts,

steeped in jars
of warm formaldehyde,

still plugged
with heartworms.

"Maybe it's a sign,"
I said. You said,

"Start asking for signs
and you'll take anything."

Green Gingko

On waking and seeing from the couch the green gingko
through the purple quills of the peacocks
sprouting out of the turquoise vase
next to the dying plant—its yellow shoots
in a sad arch—on the wooden table:

who knows where we are? Gingko leaves are
still falling, and burn has entered the air.

In the Forest

how did I make that world
disappear

      straight
       as light   the trees

growing then
bending
      so that nothing
remains
solid
         enough
    until

the dog approaches as easy as a ghost

A Curiosity

Of pond symmetries:

      you wake in a wood

of what the lake erases

tracing what are
  edge to edge
around each surface—

    •

multiplicative ponds

          —of the wood

    green song

          blue

  black

        pond—

A talking horse? You
are my companion of the road.

Place

Once, the bush was gone. Now,
the bush was gone again.

So much singing
came from the valley

as if it had always been.
There was one tree.

Its bark had many knobs.
As yellow dusk-light

clumped in the hollow
a villager stood on the hill.

It's quiet now
and dark as a wick.

About the Author

Credit: Sarune Zurba

Jordan Zandi grew up in the rural Midwest, and in 2011 graduated with an MFA in poetry from Boston University, where he was the recipient of a Robert Pinsky Global Fellowship to Bolivia. His work has appeared in *The New Republic, Little Star, The Laurel Review*, and *Bluestem Online.* He lives in Indiana with his wife and their two rabbits.

Acknowledgments

The epigraphs for this book's four sections come, respectively, from William Faulkner's *Absalom, Absalom!*, Peter Reich's *A Book of Dreams*, Søren Kierkegaard's "Eternal Happiness, Subjectivity, and Truth," and Mike Dash's *Smithsonian.com* article "For 40 Years, This Russian Family Was Cut Off From All Human Contact." "The Flavor Suite" contains as epigraph a sentence from James Joyce's *Finnegans Wake*, and the epigraph for "Le Monde Familier" is a line from Wallace Stevens's "The Auroras of Autumn." The title of the poem "The Circus in Winter" is borrowed from Cathy Day's historical novel of the same name; this poem also contains a line from Ezra Pound's "Canto LXXXI," along with a verse, Job 4:15, from the King James Bible.

I am grateful to the editors of the magazines in which poems from this manuscript were previously published, sometimes in slightly different forms: *The New Republic* ("Solarium"), *Little Star* ("Chamber Music," "Snow Children"), *The Laurel Review* ("On My Pony Life," "On My Plane Life"), and *Bluestem Online* ("On Stepping off the Train," "From a Bridge").

I would like especially to offer thanks to the following people and institutions: to Boston University, the Elizabeth Leonard Fellowships, and the Robert Pinsky Global Fellowships, which provided time; to Robert Pinsky and Rosanna Warren, who gave much helpful feedback; to Sarah Gorham, who helped with final edits; to Sarabande Books, who put this book on shelves; to Henri Cole, who chose it in the first place; to Ken Armstrong, a kid's first reader; to Thom Satterlee, my first model of a writing life; to Rebecca van Laer, for shrewd counsel; to Aaron Kerner and Chiara Scully, for helping to edit many of these poems at various stages of their existence; to my parents, for limitless support and for putting up with this business for so many years; to Louise Glück, with greatest thanks, who made this book more possible; and to Vilija, the companion of my life.

The Kathryn A. Morton Prize in Poetry

2013 Sean Bishop, *The Night We're Not Sleeping In*
Selected by Susan Mitchell

2012 Trey Moody, *Thought That Nature*
Selected by Cole Swensen

2011 Lauren Shapiro, *Easy Math*
Selected by Marie Howe

2010 David Hernandez, *Hoodwinked*
Selected by Amy Gerstler

2009 Julia Story, *Post Moxie*
Selected by Dan Chiasson

2008 Karyna McGlynn, *I Have to Go Back to 1994 and Kill a Girl*
Selected by Lynn Emanuel

2007 Monica Ferrell, *Beasts for the Chase*
Selected by Jane Hirshfield

2006 Gabriel Fried, *Making the New Lamb Take*
Selected by Michael Ryan

2005 Matthew Lippman, *The New Year of Yellow*
Selected by Tony Hoagland

2004 Simone Muench, *Lampblack & Ash*
Selected by Carol Muske-Dukes

2003 Karen An-hwei Lee, *In Medias Res*
Selected by Heather McHugh

2002 Carrie St. George Comer, *The Unrequited*
Selected by Stephen Dunn

2001 Rick Barot, *The Darker Fall*
Selected by Stanley Plumly

2000 Cate Marvin, *World's Tallest Disaster*
Selected by Robert Pinsky

1999 Deborah Tall, *Summons*
Selected by Charles Simic

1998 Aleida Rodríquez, *Garden of Exile*
Selected by Marilyn Hacker

1997 James Kimbrell, *The Gatehouse Heaven*
Selected by Charles Wright

1996 Baron Wormser, *When*
Selected by Alice Fulton

1995 Jane Mead, *The Lord and the General Din of the World*
Selected by Philip Levine

Sarabande Books is a nonprofit literary press located in Louisville, KY, and Brooklyn, NY. Founded in 1994 to champion poetry, short fiction, and essay, we are committed to creating lasting editions that honor exceptional writing. For more information, please visit sarabandebooks.org.